Tainted Times

(100 Days of Prose)

by
Amurá Oñaā

Published by

AMURÁ
UNLIMITED LLC

2019

Other Books by Amurá Oñaa

The Promise
(Poem)

Amurati
Vol. 1
(50 Short Stories, 300 words or less)

The Seed
(Origin of AI)

Jonathan Hood in Close the Door Behind You

The Haven House
Co-authored with Joe Hunt

Amurati
Sci-Fi & Fantasy
Vol. 2
(50 Short Stories, 300 words or less)

This is a work of poetry.

ISBN 978-0-578-62476-1

TAINTED TIMES
(100 DAYS OF PROSE)

Cover Art by Claudia Gibson-Hunter, from an excerpt of her work entitled "A Key for the Takers"

Published by Amurá Unlimited, LLC

www.amuraunlimited.com

To Those Who Step Out
From Behind Tightly Drawn Curtains
to Stand in the Light

Introduction

To be honest with you, I wanted to see if I could write one poem a day for a whole year. Well, after the initial trial run, I came to realize, with my other projects put on hold, that soon after hearing their clamor and pleading for recognition, 365 days would be a little much. After two months, I felt it would be tough enough for me to reach seventy-five, so I decided to push myself at least one hundred, starting from June 1st to September 8th of 2019.

And anyway, whoever said I was a poet, I mean a real poet, the kind I envision in my head. While I've done some song lyrics and poetry off and on in my life, I don't even feel I have the temperament to be a poet. It became a case of letting me see what I can do or write and keeping it to a one-page format.

Hence I make no claims. Maybe this process will help and inspire me to become better at this craft. There may be a few gems in this grouping, allowing me some level of growth. In my editing of the prose, I found myself taming some of the wording and toning down some of the anger out in my work, I decided to leave it as is. We experienced some tainted times during the 100 days, so I won't apologize for my pain, feelings, disappointments. or hopes.

I know, full well, that I will have to approach this again in some form at another point in my life, hoping I improve in the process.

Much of what I'm expressing is based on the reactions or thoughts to ongoing events during this period in my life, and in the lives of many sharing this timeline, some happenings conjured memories from other points in my past. One can only wonder what other unsettling events will come to light in the days following these.

The Month of June

6/1/2019

Waiting
    for too few life preservers.
        with millions like me reflected
            on the waters,
        floating between rescue and a funeral dirge.

Reason shrugs,
    and I swim below
    the surface
    of their reality.

Tis nothing (k)new, just forgotten.

Submerged
    by the way, by the path,
        by the current state of being.

Like that guy in Chap. 5, verse 13 of
    "Life of a Paramecium,"

Waiting below,
    watching the boats offering rescue
        via re-indoctrination;
            watching them sink
                from da holes in their logic.

Still, it's "Rot," the Equalizer;
    and there's more of that in the system
        then they wish to admit.

Some talk with a hunger,
    ravenous,
        Eating at and through you.

The poisonous chards
    in their speech
        numb and cause the "swoon"
            you swore you'd avoid.

You sit there,
    Skin tough but absorbent.

You nod,
    then drift
        as they weave a webbing.

They then suck
    and drain, suck, and drain.

Their pleasure?
    To leave enough for the next feeding.

Watching you stumble
    on home to sleep it off.

And you thought vampires a myth.

6/3/2019

Coughing up more
   these days.

Guess old age
   and all that surplus bullshit
      (10lbs in a 1lb bag) —
         something's got to give.

Been savin' it
   for my homies,
      we barter in BS,
         but most've gone home.

No sense passing it on
   to young folk,
      they be startin' their own
         collection.

Anyways - they can spot me comin'
   a mile off.

One sec, kah, cough, ke ka . . . hey
   gag. cough, breathe, cough, sorry,
      k - kau - never mind.

Honey, they will always
   want what you got!

   But why, Mama?

Cause they don't know
   how to get it their damn selves.

   But Mama, ain't that stealing?

Shush chile, ain't stealin'
if you ain't around
to say it stole.

Sleep!

Its music extracted,
    broken down to a chord,
       chiseled to a note.
    Then like fairy dust - released.

Thru a haze,
    you be smilin',
       and you don't know why.

They be killin', so many dyin',
    Shruggin' ya shoulders
      cause you dreamin'
        you be free.

Free to sleep, a sleep to free
    you from a swirlin' nightmare
      called Truth.
    You won't know Truth
      dreamin' of truth
        suckin' on their nipple,

Til Chaos rattles loud
    in the debri field
      called Life.

Day 5

6/6/2019

Who will sing for me?

A song I never sung
   in a language ripped
   and painted over;
   white, washed, and scrubbed

With powerful rhythms muted down
   to sun-day sidewalk hymns,
     and a two-bit tampourine
       on a hip wide with anticipation

Hoping for salvation
   that we
     never needed in the 1st place
      being pure and original,
     but to them we be 2nd class anyways;
     the kind of ugly their God don't like.

I prefers it that way.

Anyways, the song I hears
   ain't the songs they be singin'
     it be a chorus of ancestral voices
   only having to call once
     and I respond.

Bad enough
they erase you,
   then claim you
      and your works
   as theirs.

Denunciations,
   annunciations
      ingrained,
     hard boiled,
     and peppered
     with a dash of faults
   on a scrabbled mind.

Got you
   falsifying
   demystifying
   an image of self
   that would impress
     God herself.

Finding happiness?

Never met the guy.
   Worried?
      Nah.
   Concerned?
      Nah.

One day we'll meet
   with an obscure,
      unannounced,.
         passive pat on the back,
      and a stirring smile.

I mean, it is
   possible,

But for now,
   pass me that broom;
      there's a lot of shit
         needs sweepin'.

6/9/2019

As a parent,
    anticipation
        claims you,
            stacking with each child.

A gripping,
    pressured,
        factory vice
            squeezing
    out factors,
        possibilites
    they rarely flow toward.

Their path?
    The unexpected.

Their hope?
    Only that you
        show the same pride
    given on the day of their first steps
        toward you
            into waiting arms.

You be reaching,
    arms stretched
        till the ink runs dry,
            showing cracks
        on a tapestry
            etched in pain
                and colored pencils.

Arched over the excuses
    that braced your world
        keeping it from collapsing.

Praying that chance,
    called luck,
    would pull
        the shades up
    and there be
        a new day
            rising.

Only the shade
    has lost its bounce,
        grown stiff, hard, brittle,
        dark like the face
        on the other side of the glass,
        staring back at you,
            searching, but never touching.

Art to paper.
   Soul through art,
      Emotions dried and squeezed tight,
      minced and diced
         from the Spirit.

There IS no good to the last drop.

The good in something
   is for another time,
      in a spectrum of glass shards,
      emitting groans filtered by palabras
         seeking meaningless truths,
         obtruse mutterings
         that swore
            Art could be tamed by logic.

Instead, there's Nothing
   like the Vacancy
      leftover
   after the Fillings are removed,
   leaving a raw nerve
      opened to Doubt,
         the Second Guessing
            every artist is born with.

How many times
   have I walked
   a path like this?

Am I the old soul I feel I am
   or is it an illusion
   to the Nth degree?

To Be is to always
   to have been.

And this connection
   I feel to all life:
      Fairy Tale, chapter thirteen
     of "Hoping There's More to Life
        Than the Shit Laid Out Before Me."

So when I say
   I know,
   who am I
      trying to convince?
        And why should I care;
        for somehow I am Everthing
        and consciousness will flow
           back to the Source
           in one way or another.

It's the weight
   we carry
      the weight that crushes
      and holds us to a spot,
         to a place,
         or a system.

Collecting collections is a
   side-effect of the species
   (gathering dust for dust sake).
      why so hard to let go?

The greater the collection,
   the more solidification,
      prominence of presence,
   proof of being,
      if only to be remembered
         for the amount,
         the tonnage,
            not for accomplishments,
            but for all the shit
               we leave behind.

What do they want?

What is it they ask for?

Questioning,
   ever asking.
     for proof
       of identity.

Proving what?
   Manhood?
     Womanhood?

Are you that square?
   Unable to fit
     into their round hole?

Conforming.
   always rounding off your corners
     while that Red 15 watt
     flashes Reject! Reject!
     Praying through toil and sweat
     that the white 15 watt
     will go off.
       indicating you passed,

And once a cog in the machine,
   then what?

A calling,
    believed or not,
        a calling
        heard
        beneath the flannels
            of a culture
            texturally
            opposed
                to your own.

And through the fibers,
    your turned neck
        arching over
        backward
        towards your ancient yesterdays;
    for yesterdays wake you
        in whispers.

You follow
    and change course
        for you have
            no choice.

Not when
    you are not sewn
        into the fabric
            of their tomorrow.

6/16/2019

Pull together
   the lost strings
     that have lossed
    their tone,
      their vibrance.

Your song
   won't be heard
   by the stars overhead.

You're strumming
   with a sponge
     absorbing daily excuses;
   and you call yourself
    a musician,
     having yet to play
      one chord of hope!

Resting East
   of the trouble spot;
     clammering,
     believing
       there'd be a free zone
  of hospitable feelings
     where ideas would flourish,
       only to find
       that what is East
       is only West again,
   and all is infected,
      bleached, chalked,
        and dry
          from honest emotions,
    that used to hold substance,
      yet remain cracked
        from the touch,
       however slight,
       Realism has to offer.

Squeezed,
    pushed against
        the unknown
        of tomorrow.

A tomorrow you will
    willingly
        or unwillingly
            extrapulate from this stage.

These layers
    of curtains,
        keeping you
        in front of an audience
            that never applauds;
        and with each crowd
            coming from behind
            a stained-glass window
            adorned with intricate patterns
                that display
                a picture of life
                never before seen —
    causing you to raise
        your head to peer
            outside and beyond
                this universe.

6/19/2019

Mama's crying
    is scratching hard
        against the silence
            of the night.

Daddy's cutting her again
    with words
        sharp,
            angular in context.

Flesh wounds
    from his empty stance
        in their vacant room,
    but to her and her children
        cuts go deep as we listen with
            tear-stained eyes
        hidden under covers
            covering up one to another,
        masking our fear to even utter
            a sound.

It's raining hard in our house
    cause
Mama's crying
    is scratching hard
        against the silence.

What makes you think
    I'm free
        from the infection,
            the infestation,
            the indoctrination?

This boat I may have built,
    but look closely at the sail.
        raise your hand in the air,
            feel the wind,
            its direction
            where it blows to, and fro.

You can taste it
    in my expressions,
        in my choice of good
        and evil.

I am their child;
    corrupt to the marrow
        programmed to betray myself
        should I find fault
            in their lies
        I've been spoonfed
            since my mother's womb
            released me into their midst.

6/21/2019

Triggers oscillating
    cause
        we on a hand-written menu
        they never printed out.

Whose fault is that?

Mama spat,
    Time has a rhythm
    And if you can't read
        the rhythm of the times
            you livin' in,
        your ass gonna
            get whooped.
    Specially if you can't figure out
        today's specialty
            they be cookin'.
    For there be messages in the soup.
        a story in the beans,
            a consequence for the gravy.

Be no reason to the season,
    no inclination to the nation,
    no civility in their ability
        to add you to the list
        they be aching to fill
            and mark you off as M.I.A.

6/22/2019

Preparation, Reparation
Remember-ation, Segmentation -
   Costing them so much
      Cause "giving" just ain't their style;
   Only the body count matters,
      and it ain't Black lives,
   but bodies in bounty bags
      for crimes we have yet committed.

Can't find "due" in reparations,
   like there's no "guilt" in genocide.

Scale's been tipped for decades,
   stretched in their favor.
   Rusted, crusted,
      trusting that no one can sense the slant
      in their decline.

Now we want to bring balance
   to a house divided
      and pitched on a steep incline(d)
      to stay that way.

We gave too much for them
   to quantify or understand the gift,
      the loss, the pain
         of our humanity
            for their inhumanity.

Tangled
    with no space
        to breathe.

Each string pulling
    the other
        back,
    creating more knots.

Confused and mistakened,
    we called it
        love.

But love
    has its own gooey,
    pasty side.

We done tried
    a coupled couple
        hinged on the fringe
        of nothingness.

For all the effort
    we make,
    take and fake
    at being free,
        you and I -
            just a one-cell organism.

why didn't I
    make the effort to see you?
        Sharing laughs
            and memories.
    Busy?
    Doing what?
    Learning how to pass the time?
    Pulling excuses out of my ass?

Now you're gone,
    passed
        away from all
            who knew you.

Am I angry
    at the me
        who failed you?

More like dissappointed
    at a chance,
        like so many chances
    lost from our lives.

You have every right
    to laugh your ass off,
        when we meet
        on sacred ground.
        Love you.

6/25/2019

Captured again.
    How many lifetimes?
    Forever, the escape plan.
    Eternal, the rebellion.

Have I ever tasted
    the sweetness of freedom
        and salivated its flavor
        for more than a day
            at some time
            in another life,
                time, or being?

I must have
    suckled it,
        rolled it around
        in my mouth
            'til it found its way
            to my heart.

Cause I'm gonna taste it again;
    the urge is too strong;
        its taste too sweet,
            and this life too short.

Playing music
   again,
      trying to birth
        that creature
        who had wings
     to fly me
     beyond my natural
       self.

Reaching for the inner song
   that has always
      been out there
     somewhere
       within.

Playing music
   again,
      there's a smile
     on my soul,
       if only for a short time.

We
    affect the effects
        we ooze
           like so much mucus.

Noses wiped,
    brains erased
        of the sensitive shades,
        colored under
        crimes committed.

Sleeves too short
    to eleviate
        all the sins
           we coughed up.

We have a cold,
    and it has nothing
        to do with germs,
    but acts,
    sickeningly contagious.

Learning to cover
    our mouths.
    an aperture we never should've opened.

Thought we were communicating,
    our bad.

The door
   never fully open,
      hardly ever closed,
   just swinging
      to a universal breeze.

The problem?
   Not the door,
      not the ever-changing
         opening.

The problem:
   the size
      of my ego.

Forget the door,
   could I even get by
      the stone frame
         without jamming
      the entranceway for others?

It was time for dieting
   only the ratio
      of ego to frame
         remained the same.

It was never about others, anyway,
   it was always about me.

6/29/2019

The story was never about me.
    The role I played
        held no significance.

I observed,
    rarely participated,
        other than to change positions,
            viewpoints
        for nothing else but an effect
           and a better angle.

The tears I wept,
    part of a simulation
        of inclusion in this illusion.

I played the parts
    in masking
        my purpose
    as notations
        and field reports
            were cast upon the waters
              of time
           returned to Sender,

This is your story,
    never mind the man behind the curtain.
        I'm on the outside lookin' in.

6/30/2019

An impatient world,
    rushing to solve
        itself
            with a blank slate.

Hoping to avoid
    a reflection
        of a history
            colored in darkness,

A brighter future
    shadowed in grays,
        looking for any shade
            lighter than yesterday
    for confirmation
        of a prophetic path
            down a yellow-brick road.

Wanting room,
    needing forgiveness
        for the monsters
    they elected to rule over them;
        the beasts allowed to seize control.

An impatient world,
    rushing to solve
        itself
            with a blank slate.

The Month of July

7/1/2019

Stationary rhythms
    echoing off walls
    back onto itself.

I have no recollection
    of the sound,
    the tempo
    that would move my heart
        to joy,
    my soul to tears,
        always longing for a native mother's song
            for this suckling child.

My skin,
    tight,
    stretched,
    and played upon
    by souls
        full of emptiness.
    I scream at the rhythms
        pounding me
        into a sleep
            my ancestors warned me of — saying,
    "Chile, whatever you do,
        Do not close your eyes,
            Unless you're prepared to Dream!"

Everything for a reason
   reasoning being
     everything.
The walk,
    shorter than I realized
      I was part of
      the problem
      before I knew it.

Preceding birth,
   the idea of my conception
    bothered them,
   like the idea of
    my children's children.

Forget being being born in sin,
   some of us are born
     colored in their fear
      poised to burst
     every dam(n)
     thing.

For fear is a skin
   this viper
    has yet learned
     how to shed.

7/3/2019

Family,
   it's been hard to acquaint
      myself
         to them.

What's blood got to do with it.
   Like the love
      Tina be sassin' about.

Support,
   rarely seen,
   hardly shown.

Brothers and sisters
   from crib sty,
   criticizing,
      feelin' free
         to tear each other down
      placing blame
         like so much change
            on a counter in a candy store.

Love from afar
   like walkin' on eggshells,
   following protocol
      for as long as we are blind
      to strength of family
         it be workin' - for someone out there.

Day 33

7/4/2019

She knew every button,
    pushing them came easy.
Conditioned to respond,
    swearing alligiance,
        accepting the lies
        as truth,
        and truth as history.
I saluted
    the idea of freedom
    from the cage
    incasing this mind.
For I was raised
    to love her,
        programmed to submit.
Dreaming
    of the independence
        she claimed to offer;
    only to be in dependence
        of a system of shadows
            blanketing a world
                gone wrong.
Her story lost in the story of others.
Out of the mire
    stood old glory
        and in the distance I stand
            no longer able
        to look her in the eye.

7/5/2019

Stained glass eyes,
 with kaleidoscopic vision
  viewing this upside-down world
   already in motion.

Attempting to make sense
 by bringing background
  to foreground
   while skewing the haze
   and calling it clarity,

Sheepishly jumping from today
 to yesterday,
  screaming in the now
   to hear it echo
   in some tomorrow.

All while speed
 is define by the shift
  in colors
   rushing toward me
   only to eminate
   in the distance.

Where Love is felt
 in the now,
  when sharing
   was the song
   we shared with one another.

Day 35

7/6/2019

Are there any messages
    remaining?
        Any tools left
        for us to continue
        the building process
    or are the words all gone?

The instruments
    tucked away
    in a shelter
    somewhere
        off the main road.

Where are there weapons
    left to fight with
    or does one generation
        leave the next
        wanting?

For I can't remember
    the warnings,
        cause maybe
        I wasn't listening
        with all that
            hollering going on
            in the background.

Seeking answers
   while held up
      with the patterns
      in the fabric of this existence

Ever unfurling,
   showing no let up,
   no ease,
   backing me
      against walls
        I never built.

I can no longer
   see the selection
      of Mr. John's
        candy display.

I came in wanting
   two for a nickle
      only to find
      my piggy bank
      doesn't have
        the change
          they demand
          I go through.

Day 37

Brick wall,
   high
      up above my head
      I hear music;
         up on tippy toes
     for the air be clear
       on the other side.
     Still, can't see shit!

And on my side
   be murmurs
      thought it be them images
      talkin' in tongues
      only to find they be
      talkin' in shadows.

Cause spirits don't reside
   on my side,
      so I span my wings
      to let these feathers lift me
        up above my head.
   and I come to understand why
     the wall be so high;
  teach me, they did
    and I built it well.

Counting sheep,
   like my life depended on it,
   cause wolves
  be out there
    roaming,
   pass the gate draped
    in the shreds
      of misplace friendships,
      forgotten relationships,
    leaving trust
   far behind me
     out on the field of life.

Baa, baa black sheep
Three bags full
   with every drug in paradise,
    where every truth is bull!

Day 39

70+ year-long steps downward,
   deep into this dimension,
   still aint never learned
     to tame these beasts.

For they still
   be punching
   the numbers,
     fiddling with
     the programming
       while factoring out
       the ratio
         of their wants
         to our needs.

And according to them
   our needs
   must coincide
     with their wants,

And if they want us
   to kill ourselves,
   we need to kill ourselves.

Simple equation
   in their factorial configuration,
   but one crucial flaw
     in the equating of their calculations,
       we be an exponential people.

My father used to say,
   long as children are born
   life goes on.

Well dad,
   they be killin'
   children
      in every way
      possible.

Stripping this planet dry
   of our tomorrows.
   supporting the greed of others
   to hunt, starve,
   cage, imprison,
   abuse, traffic,
   exploit, chain,
   sell, enslave
      with behavior
      so barbaric
         it turns places of a caring heart
         into a waste land.

I raise my weary head
   and realize,
      Dad, life may have nothing
      to do with us after all,
         for it can go on without us
            and still be life.

To read the signs
   of the times,
      knowing that all
      this will pass
   and the universe
      will be
   as it's suppose to be —
      a flow from moment to moment
   till the tomorrows,
      stretching before us.
        collapse into the horizon.
   why does today
      hold impotance?
   Because I'm a part of it?
      Conscious, aware.
   Am I not always
      a part
        in the consciousness
          somewhere
            aware?
   Am I not this somewhere,
      even now as I write?

The waste
   in the corner
   has grown
   since last
     I noticed.

No one's been
   through here
   in ages,
     but somehow,
     from somewhere,
     the waste
       keeps accumulating.

Now the corner
   is me,
   pushed to my edges
     of my living space
       to a spot by the door.

Never knew waste
   could reach
   such a height.

Maybe I never cared enough;
   turning my back
   on all my wasteful doings;
   slumped in the heart,
     I walk out, sigh,
       and close the door.

7/14/2019

Am I my yesterday?
   Plain and simple
      in beliefs
         and knowings.

Assured in my doubts,
   that tomorrow
      holds a different man
         in my stead.

Wiser?
   Hopefully,
      with changes
         like markers,
      tattoed on my soul,
         so my Orishas
      will easily
         find me in the midst
           of this chaos.

Today recedes
   into yesterdays
      leaving me
         to move back
           into my future.

7/15/2019

Falling behind,
    the positions
        are changing,
        rearranging themselves
        neath the clutter
            of untested ideas.

Solutions,
    one held close
        to the chest,
        idolized
        by a once
            shock-proof,
            steel-caged mind,
    are held in question
    every time
    they come up for air.

Deregulated,
    they're sent back to subcommittees
    only to be shot
    full of holes,
        circumsized,
            then castrated.

Knowing all to well,
    where there is no seed,
        there is no growth.

What have I to offer?
    what service
        to those requiring
        service
            can I truely feel
            worthy of?

I am a backward man,
    with an army of yesterdays
    marching behind me,
        wanting to know
        today's orders.

The Bastille
    won't be stormed today
        for if nothing else,
        I am an honest coward.

The flesh is willing,
    but the spirit is weak,
        unconvinced that there's a purpose
        underlying the fabric
            of this existence.

I tell my yesterdays
    to make camp,
        this foxhole called life will do,
            just as good as any!

They close you down
    when you call out
        their sins behind the curtains.

They claim to know
    your crimes,
        but not their own.
    For you'll always be
        the cog in their machine,
        only revealing
        the need
            for better gears.

They rely on the curtains,
    the shadows they create,
        to hide your story,
        to draw tight
        over the whistle
            of the blower,
            waiting for the inhale
                to ensure the murmurings
                of the audience,
                the lights,
                and the truth
                    go dim.

7/18/2019

People along borders,
    those needing
        to cross.
    those keeping them
        from crossing.

Tension squeezing
    them onto a wall
    that was never there
        in the first place.

Along a border
    painfully tinted in brownish hues,
    painted with a brush
        dipped in porous fear
        and sketched
        to proportions
            that suit an ill-tempered artist.
            draped in keystone-cop attire,
            pretending the buck
                stops with the orange-faced clown
                    inside a one-ring circus
                    under a white canopy
                        some mistakingly call
                        The White House

Some believe
    they need to raise
        their voice
        to be heard.

That to be noticed,
    in the midst
        of their moment
        of injustice,
        is important.

As if being vocal
    will resolve
        the issue.

Forgetting the power
    of acting in silence;
        achieving the means
        by carefully coordinating
            a series of acts
            to produce
            the required outcome.

I won't argue against
    the strength of voice,
        for some get to be
        seen and heard
        with Ego demanding recognition,
            still . . . use wisely.

No time to be wasted on politics,
   for politics
     be a waste of time.

Hallowed halls can-sprayed in ignorance
   adorned in worn, torn, delapidated drapes
     knocking out
     the light of reason,
     while wisdom, along with justice
       ride neath the broom
       of the night janitor.

Swept into bins
   to fuel a furnace fire
     ignited with Tiki torches
     waved by soulless,
       banshee racists
       ritually swirling themselves
       in a nonsensical dance
       of maniacal dominoes
         falling into a pattern
         resembling hatred.

No time for politics,
   just wipe your ass
     and find something
       productive to do.

7/21/2019

Taking chances
     with stress inhibitors
     making mirrored mimes
          to tell our story
          and express our reality.

Nerves nearing
     nucleus disruption
     cause chaos
          fabricates
          fraudulent
          fibers
          only to shread
               when "can,"
               merges with "do."

And performance
     withers in the light
     on the stage.

Living with every
     false truth,
     until we become
          comfortable
          with the laughter
          of the universe.

Rain caught me,
    drenched deep
    my environment,
    and water logged
    every tangible thought
        that flowed
        through me,

Only thing I could do
    or be
    was a filter
    for the soil
        that had collected,
    for the debri's
        still clogged
            in the system.

Only thing I could
    hope for
    was something
    pure
        at the bottom
        near the drain.

Still waiting,
    listening
        to the flush in the pipes.

7/23/2019

Knee deep
　　in circumstances
　　blocking, obstructing
　　　　our chances to recoup.

Are we able
　　says the master
　　to move beyond
　　　　this numbing nonsense
　　　　that keeps us tied
　　　　and chained,
　　　　chained and tied
　　　　　　to targeted areas
　　　　　　with x marking spots
　　　　　　and spots marking us?

We spend all our
　　todays on yesterdays
　　cleaning up dysfunctional debri
　　　　so tomorrow
　　　　will offer something more
　　　　than the present
　　　　　　yesterday had to offer.

Yes, we are able,
　　even willing,
　　until we read
　　　　the list of necessary
　　　　　　sacrifices.

Demented dimensional
   districts distract
   dem denizens
      of da deep
      long enough
   for pledged paranoids
   to pick da pockets
   of a paralyzed populace
   purposefully programmed
   to precede parades
      like circus clowns
      circling a circumference
         of circumstances
      of sizzling subterfuge
         stirring citizens
      into creative chaos.

Demented democracies
   demonstrating disasterous
   distractions of
      disembodied demagogues
      dysfunctionally directing
         the course of our civilization.

Reason resounds
    in the halls where we reside
       hoping it will ooze off walls
       in a civile-sticky slime
       to be absorbed
         by at least some of us.

Hopefully incapsulating the youth
    huddled beneath
    the myths and lies
       told from wash-n-rinsed-dried parents
       cautioning offspring to stay
         out of harm's way.

But to hear youth
    speaking pearls,
    offerimg consultation, and guidance
    to those of us misplaced along
       a path of promises
       Ancestors did their best to steer us toward.

For within those pearls
    in the midst of harm's way,
    hope renews itself
       and pride finds a place
       in our hearts;
         enough to keep us from falling over.

Causes,
    provoking circumstances
    for no thing
      is stationary.

This medium
    we reside,
      most volatile;
    there's more of the unseen,
      than the seen
      never taking credible form,

An unearthy
    fog whisping
      at our feet
    never taking shape,
      but always
    assuming a presence,
    initiating situations affecting all.

The cauldron is alway stirring,
    for spell(ing) is eternal.
    Thoughts are things,
      words - creatures,
        ravenous, and savage.

Who knew our speech,
    our pets,
      held such venom.

I feel the weight,
   of my burden pressing down.

No need to pass it on,
   others be adding to
   their own baggage.

Personalizing their precious shit,
   claiming braggin' rights,
   "This is my shit!"
     "Stay away from my shit!"

Never coming to terms
   or a desire
     to teach others how to
     discard, downsize,
     minimalize, departmentalize,
     compress 'til
     a gem is achieved.

Don't give from your bottom,
   take from your top
     and pass it on!

Help loosen the load.

Day 57

7/28/2019

In symbols
    we find ourselves
    marked, locked and centered
    on fitting, following
    and living up to
    and within the parameters
        of those symbols.

We have been damaged
    by symbol makers
    who quantify our value
    with symbols which damage us
    thru lack of their understanding
        the origins
        of our visions
        or our intertwining roles
            in the fabric of Life.

Some are learning
    how to corrode
    the symbol-makers'
    cryptograms from within
    only to unveil
    Living Totems
        left by those
        who loved us.

Hail the corrosion!

Folks gadgetized,
   unable to turn away
   from fantasy fed,
   condensed coding,
     digitized data
        conformed to conform.

Friends trending
   friends following,
   more important
     than actual
     "in-your-face"
       friends talking
       in healing,
         supporting tones.

It's all key pressed,
   homogenized,
   numerical, fact-checking
     of fake, fictional
       yesterdays
     that never happened,
       but always believed.

It's in the nature of the gadget
   to print you out in black and gray tones,
     to keep you in their definition
       of reality.

Haven't forgotten
   debts owed.
    Patience warrants
      I stand my ground
      and confess my sins
      to brothers and sisters
        I never knew.

There must be
   a promise
   left unkept,
    a deed
    unfulfilled.

Because
   their eyes
   tear up
     for reasons
     behnd the unexplained atrocities
       by those
       unworthy to stand in our midst.

If nothing else,
   I owe them
    a better,
      unprocessed me.

7/31/2019

Timing is everything
    like pods we sprout
    an unchecked hatred for ourselves
    flowering outward
        in every conceivable
        direction,
            covering
            every talent,
            every gift
            on every path traveled.

For to love them
    must be to hate each other,
        and we won't claim
        what we don't know,
        what we refuse to accept.

The invisible flower
    we refuse to see
    but so willingly polynate,
    a culture set on automatic,
        set on betrayal,
        if not on ourselves
        to those close enough,
            an allergy we find ourselves sickened with
                at some point in our season
                    of being.

The Month of August

What is that four-letter word
   that use to drive
   us at each other's throats?
     LOVE?

Oh yeah,
   where mass confusion,
   misdirection,
   layer upon layer
     of bullshit
       foaming its way up to one's neck.

Hatred is, was, and will always be
   so simple,
   straightforward,
   concrete,
     pure.

We know
   the pay out,
   cash-n-carry,
   getting your money's worth;
     unlike Love -
       it's in the mail,
       you'll get it when you see it,
       you get what you give, crapola.

Still . . .

Life, show us
    the blessing
    that you are.

We had to be
    a part of Something,
    no matter
    what form
        No-thing took.

Through It's being
    we be,
    the gift,
    the blessing
        has always been
        in place.

Not as a reward
    It simply Is
    and for being
    we share in the Infinite

Form as the Life Force
    forever vibrating into other forms,
    beings ever becoming Being.

Forget the Heaven
    or the Hell,
        we are blessed.

8/3/2019

A source
  of our madness?

There are blind spots
  in this fabric;
  very few see
  the cosmic weave.

People consumed
  with the
  Pattern of the Patch
  the who,
  the what,
  the where,
    the match . . . ing
      pieces in the game.

The vibrations
  of inner twines,
  ushering outward a cosmic melody
  played by the Master Weaver / Musician.

So concerned with
  the few loose threads
  they never see
    or even envision
      the Tapestry
        before them.

8/4/2019

Two homeland massacres,
    violence seeping its way
        to the core
    of a nation gone more sour.

Where only the sounds
    of rapid fire
    pursuing rapid feet
    can resolve questions
        that torment
        hearts lusting for chaos
            as an answer
            to a spoon-fed hatred
            wishing to manifest
                itself
                and be recognized
                as part of our consiousness.

Well, now we see you
    for what you are.

So many pregnant
    with hate,
        giving birth.

More than likely
    we'll see you again,
        cause you only in your infancy.

8/5/2019

Poeting,
   prose-castinating,
   tracking and tackling notes
   amongst word harmonics,
       turning logic into a melody
           this elder can feel comfortable with.

There'd be distant mountain ranges,
   woodlands,
   landscapes,
   coastlines streaming words
       in magical
       imagery,
           stirring those "cherished memories,"
           long-forgotten during a time
               another life must've offered.

Writing to lie,
   to fabricate,
   to heal,
       just for the sake of it.
   To color in my grays,
       making tomorrows
           more vibrant
               if only
                   in tipid watercolors.

8/6/2019

You are intertwined
    with this planet,
    but you want
        to leave,
        to settle
        on a stage
        not meant for you.

Where there will be
    no natural acclimation.

Artificial acclimation
        for artificial humanity.

You spend time
    proving there's no need
        for connection
        to each other,
        much less this world.

You lie about
    separateness,
    of being special,
    above and beyond.

This planet spent its existence
    preparing herself
        for you, but you
            never prepared yourself
                for her.

8/7/2019

The landscape,
   an unsettling picture
      of uneducated,
      unaware,
      self-loathing,
         zombiefied husks
      groovin'
      to unidentifiable music
         or rather music
            offering no identity.

And as I work my way
   thru this mine field,
      maze of a wasteland,
   people be callin' me out
      to play n' socialize.

I only see
   muted gray-figured silouettes,
      with pens and ledgers
         tallying the wreckage,
            verifying the bodycount,
               authenticating the process.

Sorry, but I'm just too busy
   for play time.

8/8/2019

Spirit
    would try to have
        an understanding of them;
    to reach a common ground.

But while my spirit
    seeks balance,
        their's seek superiority.

Mind
    would want
        to discover
        the flaws,
        so that healing
            can take place.

But while my mind
    desires healing
        their's seek a reason
        for genocide.

Body
    wants to share
        this earth.

Their's want to own it.

And you wonder why
    I'm leary.

As much as you see,
   as much as you hear,
     there are those
     trying to sprout
     above the fumes
     reaching for dreams
       forgotten.

Lookin' over
   your shoulder
     for dark clouds
     gaining,
   feelin' the acid rain
     fall over the screams
     shrouding a conjured madness.

Only to realize
   its poisonousness,
     and though
     you rinse
     and towel dry.
       you realize —

You can't live
   in the belly of the beast
     and expect to be left untainted.

8/10/2019

They kill their own,
    willingly,
    without reservation,
    hesitation,
    and we watch
    knowing the deal,
    the circumstance,
    the reason behind
    decisions keeping
    their toxicity
        undercover.

Corruption,
    like the wayward bubbles
    in seltzer water
    rising to the surface,
        is effervescent
    leaving us to believe —

As they do theirs
    claiming necesity,
    they'll do us
        on G.P.

So if you see me,
    don't provoke me with,
        "You seem tense."

8/11/2019

Why should brown skin eagerly
    bring lies to their throats.
        reformatting their yesterdays?

Have they lost
    so much
    of themselves
    that shame
        keeps them on
        a lower level
            unwilling to rise?

I have no desire
    to stand
        in their consequence,
    for their fear
        of me and mine
            has left them
                undefinable.

For to define
    my nature
        in relationship
        to their
            current mode
            would only
                be moving backwards.

79   Day 72

You can drop
   your pants,
      but you can't raise
         your consciousness.

Reveal to yourselves your gift,
   a truth,
   a genius
      they never knew
      you had
         and you were too afraid
         to show.

There is more to you
   than pyramids,
      a sphinx,
         or buried treasures.

Move beyond the confines
   of this culture.

Show them your mysteries
   and surprise yourselves.

8/13/2019

Have you shared
    your gifts?

Have you looked
    into the night sky
    and realized
        your place amongst things?

How complaints
    from specs like us
        are unfounded
            in the majesty
            of it all.

Complainng about
    what life has done
        to you
        while you give for self
            and not to Self.

Discover
    the you by doing,
    and surrender your gifts,
        for it is by giving
            you receive.

8/14/2019

walking through
    this abyss
        in disbelief.

what are we doing
    to each other
        on this planet?

This urge for profit,
    consuming
    overflowing onto ourselves,
    slurping up the residue
    rather than
        sharing the wealth.

Greed's willingness to destroy
    the circle,
    to implode,
        then validate
            the implosion.

when you're full,
    you're no longer hungry,
        but they're never full.

OK

OK

OK

Your need to lie
    to the world?
        To yourselves?

Were we supposed
    to be
    captivated,
        enamered
            by the constant bullshit?

Aren't you proud
    of your achievements?

Haven't you done enough
    like others around the globe?

You don't have to lay claim
    to virtually everything.

Because you came late
    to the ancients
        doesn't give you
        cart blanche to rewrite
        and destroy the stories of others
            only to take credit
                where credit was never due.

Discovering the discovered.

I should expect
  what from you?

I know that
  I can't take you at your word,
    based on the history
      of what you do.

Have you not noticed
  the trail of blood
    following every
    step you take,
  the ransacked lives,
    and mounds
      of corpses
      left smoldering
        in your wake?

Your manner of persuasion —
  promises never kept,
    treaties never honored,
  disrespecting your own,
    much less the rest of us.

So tell me again,
  I should expect
    what from you?

Other than the worst,
  absolutely nothing.

8/17/2019

Thoughts locked and sealed,
    facing those who wave goodbye
        though a haze
            leaving me numb,
            out of place,
                because we no longer
                share the same space,
                time, or relationship.

There's been a shift
    with our worlds
        now out of alignment;
    she in hers, me in mine.
        Am I missing her,
            the once in a blue-moon friendship,
            and our mix,
            the melody that played
            when words flowered our conversations
            and laughter bubbled like a brook?
                Yes!

All I have now is memory,
    so memory of you will have to get me
        through my tomorrows.
            See you then.

                (To A, V, H.)

8/18/2019

Many look only to see
    a reflection
        of ignorance.

A mirror image
    of a time
    my father warned me of,
    when people
    overloaded
        with information
        would jumble it
        in a chaotic process
            back into the "real" world
            where sense,
                truth, facts, etc.
            would be prefixed
                by "non," "un,"
                and "fake."

Well, Dad,
    blessed are those
        of you resting
            with simple truths,
        even simple lies.

We got the
    M.A.G.A. bullshit.

Sound and fury
　　saturating the space
　　around this note,
　　　　this vibratory string.

I cannot discern
　　the sound,
　　　　but I can taste it -
　　　　this acidic, caustic,
　　　　　　corrosive drone,
　　　　a temporal swarm
　　　　of locust unseen,
　　　　　　devouring the melodies
　　　　　　　　around me.

I can't submit,
　　I won't succumb
　　to a chord strummed,
　　　　with no harmony
　　　　in mind,
　　　　　　with no mind
　　　　　　in the harmonics,
　　　　　　just a furious,
　　　　　　　　continuous noise,
　　　　　　deafening the souls
　　　　　　　　of all those
　　　　　　　　　　above the planet's core.

I'll rise until this note breaks
　　or the noise fades!

8/20/2019

Reason claims
    the uselessness
        of hatred
        for there is
            no focal point.

A virus
    too contagious,
        too wide spreading.
    consuming
        at a pace
            uncontrollable.

And though
    the spirit be troubled
        by those walking
        such a winding path
            which holds no destination
        worthy of this gift.

Whenever anger arises,
    I find myself drenched
        in a pathetic sadness
            for the hollowness
                of those
                who refuse to share
                    in the wonders
                        of diversity.

The drone
   of silence,
   ebbing
     from the background.,
   becoming
     louder
than the world's gasp
     of those children starving
from the callous whim
     of injustice.

In the light
   of the landscapes
     of Yemen,
echoed in
     a wicked House of Mirrors,
revealing a reflection
     with no resolve,
allowing thousands to die,
     where enough flashing lights
       has everyone
       going in
         and going out,
       thinking
         it's a carnival.

Blues be changing
   on me, and in me,
      colors don't match
   the mood,
      stress be catering
   to kaleidoscopic
      motifs
         in plaid and paisley
           configurations.

Blues ain't
   what it used to be
      with me
         laughing at the downs
         and distrusting of the ups.

Nah, blues ain't
   what it used to be,
      think I got a God complex.

8/23/2019

Walking,
  marching,
  standing up
    for toxic aberrations
    claiming to have
      your best interests
      in mind.

Convincing you
  their best interests
    was yours all along,
      and you fell for it
      like bricks tied tight,
        pulling you under.

Arms twisted,
  face to the wired-frosted glass
    that keeps you
    from viewing
      with clarity.

They got you blinking
  in your thinking,
    cause the images
      be like frosted flakes,
        sweet with no substance.

8/24/2019

Having answers —
   so many.

Asking questions —
   too few.

We pride ourselves in the knowing,
   when it is the unknowing
      we should strive for.

Those with the data
   try to outshine
      those with a heart.

Explaining the existence
   out of existence.

Self is content with those
   wondering round the center,
      seeking the center.

8/25/2019

Panting
   like he ran
      100 yard dash,
   gasping
      while trying to reclaim
      lost words
         he let loose
         without guidance,
         with no thought in mind.

Glimpsing at a horizon
   where rumors
      are most likely to rise,
      sihlouetted 'gainst a rising sun;
      where birds be chirping
         the wrong message,
         causing chaos
         to sputter and geyser up;
         leaving folks to wonder
         (like it's the ninth wonder of the world)
            taking photos
            and posting
            so social media
               will demonify you
               for farting
                  from your mouth!

Amazon jungle burning,
   man involved,
      cause he be the cause.

So concerned with the pocket
   and filling it
      to a brim, near a rim of stupidity.
         Claiming cents for sense,
         cause we got this -
         can't stand those native people
            anyways.

Science, a waste of someone's
   time and money —
      for it ain't a tragedy
      'til they say it so,
         so let them handle it.

Hate was the spark
   that set a blaze of indifference.

Mother (Earth)
   should know better
      than to leave her welfare
         in the hands
         of children.

8/27/2019

Sorry, I can't forget,
   it's not that I want to remember.

It's the environment,
   the terrain,
     the soil, the air,
       the fumes of lead-based tap water,
       the brick and mortor.

You can rub the hatred
   between your finger tips.
     and feel its crude texture.

Wetting your lips
   only adds to the taste
     in your mouth;
     death and its legacy,
     a history of injustice
       leading to a trail of tears.

I am saturated in its yesterdays,
   for it stretches
     into the lineage of all my tomorrows.

This ongoing, stagnate,
     unwavering mist of inhumanity
       has nothing to do with memory,
     it is here, before me,
       whenever I open my eyes.

The cries of babes
   be running folks
     up the wall,
   cause youngins
     ain't understanding
  what should already
     be understood.
  And we don't have time
     to explain,
        when raising them against the clock.

Thinkin' "grow up"
   means "speed up,"
  so we hurt 'em
  cause they can't keep the pace —
     a pace that be killin' us.

In a rush to have 'em,
   with not enuff time to cherish 'em,
  in a rush to bring 'em up
    and raise 'em on out
      of our lives.

Some be mistakes,
   blind lust, thrusting us into
     so many of us
        already crashing at the speed of life
          with no seat belt, no brakes,
           and no one to hold on to.

8/29/2019

Using people
    to the point
        of sucking out
        all your wealth
            paid with their lives drained.

Concerned only
    with gross profit margin,
    and death
        a willing price
        to pay
        to block out the memory
            of their suffering.

Knowing someone,
    (according to the beliefs
        you fed them)
    must be punished
    for the guilt and evil
        of your misdeeds,
    while knowing they deserved
        a greater potion
    of your wealth —
        The punishment
            that justly belongs to you,
            you place on them.

Claiming these people are
    the uncivilized ones,
        the savages.

8/30/2019

Morals whithering,
   basic respect
      hitting rock bottom;
      sirens, once mythical,
      wail throughout the nite
         cause people tense,
         be intensely hurting one another.

And freak shows are now
   a common occurance,
      cause venting, like breathing
      is a normal function.

For there's enough obscene indifference
   to keep one's mind occupied.
      and even preocupied
      should the need arise to forget
         the circus and the misdemeanors.

Everyone is so busy
   writing the last act
      for this show.

Standing within the storm,
   the swirling hyprocrisy,
     slashing
     tall structures,
     leaving hope
       huddled underground,
     only to find
       shelter non-existent.

Eyes shut tight
   against flying debri
     from dreams
   sifted too fine
     to qualify
     as having any
       worth or value.

Blind storm raging
   sightless in its dynamo
     leaving a trail of darkness,
       and those claiming to see,
       call out false truths,
       deafened by its roar.

The Month of September

9/1/2019

Calling into rememberance
　　those who stood
　　　　by me, when most thought
　　　　it would be better to go.
　　　　　　Too much shit
　　　　　　already stuck
　　　　　　　　to the bottom of their shoes.
　　　　　　Feelin' safe
　　　　　　creating a distance —
　　　　　　　　at least
　　　　　　　　until my passover was clear.

It was in those tipid and shallow times,
　　they spoon-fed me
　　what little nourishment
　　　　my spirit yearned,
　　　　but was too proud to ask.

They knew me better
　　than I knew my self,
　　having the patience
　　　　to let me heal,
　　having the wit and sass
　　　　to keep me on my feet,
　　　　ducking and dodging
　　　　　　the pitfalls
　　　　　　they knew
　　　　　　　　were still along my path.

Good, loving friends.

Impatience becomes me —
   fooled myself into believing
      we were an intellingent species,
      holding promise —
         there are not enough Christs
         to wipe away the sins
         of one generation,
            let alone those passed since.

They label without understanding value,
   unless when it suits them.

So many planning
   the downfall of so many.

Truth being sacrificed
   every time it walks the street
   nailed to billboards
      in subway stations
   so express riders
      can get a quick glimpse,
      and shake their heads
      as eyes avoid the reality
         of their reality.

Maybe, it's me —
   too many bad days in a row
      of too many rows.

Words?
   They be scattering about,
     hiding behind pillars and posts,
     peeking with antennae eyes
       scampering to new cracks
       in my psyche.

Sometimes they can't be found,
   I mean, it's not like
     I want to find them.
   sit down with them
     and exchange specifics
     or credentials.

Some I haven't seen in ages,
   others I rarely ever meet,
     at least only in far off rumors.

Can I call myself a writer,
   if words don't come
     knockin' at my door?
   Obviously I'm not their greatest fan.

It's a buffet
   and I'm in the wrong diner.

Still, once in a while,
   they'll play a game
     of tag,
     where I'm always it.

The day's end.
   people either making
   or breaking promises,
      responsibilities,
        lying to themselves
           to extend deadlines.

Observing obligations,
   reaching deep
      for that extra pound of flesh
      to stay above the fray
        one sec longer than everyone else,
      expressing disappointments
        with others,
      making sure someone shares their pain,
        even if they don't know why.

Others dealing out happiness,
   kindness, comfort,
      like cards from a pile of 52-pick-up..

Why I should expect anything
   more than the daily struggle,
      expressed by all living things,
        is beyond me.

I suppose I listened
   to one too many fairytales.
      Youth can be so damaging.

A Healing Song
    is required,
        one not song with words,
    nor vibrating through strings
        or blown through pipes
            and instruments of wind,
    but from the ancient drums
        within.

Drums that gave rise
    to the universe itself —
        Heartbeat of heartbeats.

A song long forgotton —
    One of spirit and understanding
        played by all the stars,
        and their offspring,
        the melody heard in constellations
            and echoed amongst the galaxies.

Renew the song,
    awaken and return the dance,
        rekindle the sight
        to look beyond
            the Fog of Illusion,
                this Mist of Deception.

One comes to realize
    that to stare
    into the abyss
        and expect an answer
        that offers light,
            resilience,
            and hope
            is foolish.

The world of shadows
    offers little
    but the wisdom
    to seek answers elsewhere.

Too much time spent
    on the disease and not the cause —
    after all, it is the wicked
        we find entertaining,
    the sickness
        that turns the stomach,
    reaching inward
        to plant memories
            along the walls of our civilization.

Turn toward that simple flame
    in the darkness,
    that whispered, musical tone against the silence,
        that petal gliding in the wind,
            the snowflake angling toward your nose
            and be refreshed by life's majesty.

Thoughts turned to family,
    this day echoing
        parents sharing lives in 1946,
      a mother's father's
        day of entering this realm as well.

A parents' blending of souls
    becoming the pathway
      for my form.

They are here,
    and no longer here,
      for I breathe in their loving memory,
      still trying to understand
      our connections —
    the fabric of their stories
      issuing out mine,
      complex and incomplete
      yet closer to its end
        than yesterday.

Of grandfather
    I knew little,
    of parents I only have a fraction
      of what I wanted to know.

No one tells the child
    to pay attention
      to the details
        for it is gone, before the lesson is over.

The door swings close
    only to open
        on the other side.
    What is it in me
        that believes things will change
            for the better?

Sadly, too many sermons
    about keeping one's head
        to the sky.

Still, I can't surrender,
    must keep turning pages —
    can't quit when the story
        grows stormy,
        that's a dream for me and mine
        others would prefer,
            but it just won't do.

For now,
    I'll draw the blinds,
    turn to fade
        and retreat into the shadows of my room
        for some required rest,
        close these weary eyes,
        and after a peaceful run,
        open them,
        stretch til the blood flows,
        only to rise,
            and continue this story
                on the other side of the door.

Day 100

About the Author

Self-portrait of artist as a young man, currently in his early seventies. Form is nothing without the spirit expressing itself in words, music, and art. It's there, in the creative process, that I am visible, one soul to another. Thank you for taking in some of my thoughts at a point in my life.

www.ingramcontent.com/pod-product-compliance
Lightning Source LLC
Chambersburg PA
CBHW060445040426
42331CB00044B/2629